Nostos

Nostos

V. Penelope Pelizzon

OHIO UNIVERSITY PRESS

ATHENS

Ohio University Press, Athens, Ohio 45701
© 2000 by V. Penelope Pelizzon
Printed in the United States of America
All rights reserved

Ohio University Press books are printed on acid-free paper ⊗™

10 09 08 07 06 05 04   6 5 4 3 2

Library of Congress Cataloging-in-Publication Data
Pelizzon, V. Penelope.
    Nostos / V. Penelope Pelizzon.
       p.   cm.
    ISBN 0-8214-1298-1 (acid-free paper). — ISBN 0-8214-1299-X
(pbk. : acid-free paper)
    I. Title.
PS3566.E385N67   1999
811'.54—dc21   99-36767
                                                        CIP

Acknowledgments

I would like to thank the editors of the journals in which some of these poems first appeared:

ARK/Angel: "Tahoe City Hello Girls"
Five Fingers Review: "The Body of Speech and Silence"
The Formalist: "The Wedding Day"
Gulf Coast: "To a Paleolithic Boy in His Grave" and "Earliest Church"
The Iowa Review: "The Better Half of Man" (as "The Flower Called I Want")
The Kenyon Review: "The Feast of San Silvestro"
Midlands: "How to Get to Sleep"
The Nation: "A Late Apostasy"
Ploughshares: "Clever and Poor" and "They Lived Here"
The Southern Review: "The Mind Descending From Above" and "Adagio Ma Non Troppo"
ZYZZYVA: "The Keeper" (as "Keeping")

Thanks also to my teachers and colleagues at the University of Massachusetts-Boston, the University of California at Irvine, and the University of Missouri. I am grateful for funding from these universities, as well as for a Jacob K. Javits Fellowship, which provided financial support while many of these poems were written. Special thanks to Lynne McMahon and Rod Santos—stern preceptors, ideal readers, endless sources.

For my family
and in memory of my father:

An ancient riddle asks
What is that thing which nightly digs
through the ruins of the abandoned village?
And the attentive child answers, *The heart.*

Contents

III.

IV. Nostos

The Mind Descending from Above

What have they to do with love's bleakest shapes,
these radiantly formed and tinted tropic fish
pouting, flirting, veiling themselves with pleated fans,
artfully poised as end-of-season debutantes?
The question might never surface in the mind
did not the stenciled pet-shop window filled with tanks
proffer their silvered, variously saline worlds
below a sign for family and couples therapy

offered in a suite upstairs. So hot-tongued spouses
cooling towards divorce, and helplessly infertile couples
burning to be blessed, and parents whose adolescents
smolder in hormonal rage are all met walking up,
then fifty minutes later coming down, with box on box
on box of water and its abstract occupants.
And what have these to do with love?
Everything, in the mind descending from above.

The mind descending is distinguished, not
by sorrow since that's every place, but by its self-
projected metaphors, finding its own poses
enacted in each tank. What better illustration
of fixation on a failed romance than the tedious
glass-to-glass sweeping of the *Dracula Plecostomus*?
Nostalgia embodied, its aimless and feeble circling
hardly shimmers its shroud-like, midnight tail.

Another mind might recognize its shadow
showing through the *Bloodfin Tetra*'s opal sides.

Despite red smudges darkening its dorsal edges,
each tiny fish is so sheer-skinned its bladder
glows, milky as a barium x-ray illuminating
years of swallowed guilt. And the *Pineapple Swords*—
there must be jealous minds among that school
darting and sparring in vivid thrusts. What imagined

infidelities avenged by their barbed dueling stripes?
Today, the tank of the *Large Jack Dempsey*
and the *Medium Jack Dempsey* is empty.
Have they died or did someone buy them?
Flushed, or flashing elsewhere in a brand-new tank,
a fishy domesticity with freshly graveled floors of pink
and a little plastic diver who bobs and strews
pearl-ropes of oxygen from his bathyspheric hood?

What could the mind extend to match those pearls?
Bereaved, repeating once-learned phrases
newly understood—*"water cools not love"*—
one mind finds beside the Dempseys' crossed-out names
a rack displaying aquarium hobbyist magazines.
The first promotes *Marine Gastropods:*
Practical Snails for Your Kit, as if the liquid realm
most benefits when prudence anchors it.

But for this human mind and its imprudent world,
its terrestrial-yet-fluid life, what self-defining mooring
besides the empty glass? Perhaps this absence
proves the earlier conjecture wrong:
                                        reflection,
not projection, defines the mind descending from above.
Is that why the mind finally leaves the ghostly

Dempseys' vacant tank, and passes down fluorescent
bubbling aisles? It feels what it sees,

and is drawn to a standstill before the smallish
Gold-Piece Mollies. Despite their name—
suggesting clannish tartan lasses armed with flintlocks
hijacking the highland stage—they're not much to look at.
Maybe at some forgotten evolutionary point
their modest dust of shining scales lay thicker.
But they possess a confidence of motion,
neither splenic dashing nor dully gaping catatonia,

which balances the water's fluctuating currencies
of weight and salt and temperature. The mind absorbs
their steady tolerance to fingers tapping on the glass.
A scotch-taped card announces that the Mollies
are on sale this week, "priced special" at ninety-nine cents
for two. What mind descending could afford to miss—
if not buying, at least seeing—the attentive, gently testing
gestures of this once-flamboyant, least-expensive fish?

I

Clever and Poor

She has always been clever and poor,
　　especially here off the Yugoslav train

on a crowded platform of dust. Clever was
　　her breakfast of nutmeg ground in water

in place of rationed tea. Poor was the cracked
　　cup, the missing bread. Clever are the six

handkerchiefs stitched to the size of a scarf
　　and knotted at her throat. Poor is the thin coat

patched with cloth from the pockets
　　she then sewed shut. Clever is the lipstick,

Petunia Pink, she rubbed with a rag on her nails.
　　Poor nails, blue with the cold. Posed

in a cape to hide her waist, her photograph
　　was clever. Poor then was what she called

the last bills twisted in her wallet. Letter
　　after letter she was clever and more

clever, for months she wrote a newspaper man
　　who liked her in the picture. The poor

saved spoons of sugar, she traded them
    for stamps. He wanted a clever wife. She was poor

so he sent a ticket: now she could come to her wedding
    by train. Poor, the baby left with the nuns.

Because she is clever, on the platform to meet him
    she thinks *Be generous with your eyes*. What is poor

is what she sees. Cracks stop the station clock,
    girls with candle grease to sell. Clever, poor,

clever and poor, her husband, more nervous
    than his picture, his shined shoes tied with twine.

Little Picaresque

Bantering in foreign tongues, my mother roamed
      across Europe seeking an "artist's life,"
  and for a few years she found one: her Gorizian cousins'
        chalk wine glinted in the bottle, friends
from the newspaper dropped by on their way to Stresa
      or Bari. This morning she started the oil sketch
resting on the easel. She describes what she plans for the
                      shadows
      suggested in loose-shouldered strokes: Roman arch
dark above a staircase; descent to a harbor scaled with sun.

Had you been fortunate enough to find yourself
      among the constellation of intimates each evening
  converging on her room, you would have found it
      impossible to imagine the city without her
poised at its center, her carved-milk legs
      crossed on a pillow, one overlooked umber smudge
tagging the wing of her hand.
                  Forty years later,
      you would recall her laughter rising effortlessly
over noises carried through the open window.

    The voices of children.
    The rattle of their bicycles passing her house.

The Wedding Day

They drove to Grado in a borrowed car,
in borrowed clothes and borrowed shoes. She drove,
pink scarf instead of flowers in her hair
while he peeled blood oranges to prove
No voice cries out, and fed each segment to
the solemn child behind, whose tiny gloves
stayed folded in her lap. His daughter, new
to him and still unsure if this is love
he offers in the form of oranges.
Who wins the mother wins the child, he croons
falsetto. *Hey, you know what stubborn is?*
It's going on your parents' honeymoon
refusing Dad a grin. He mocks a scowl—success!
His wife's smile ghosted on the smaller face.

Luna di Miele (The Honeymoon)

Just after the New Year's turn
when storms had paralyzed the roads

—schools closed, offices closed,
impossible even getting to

the city, though we could see it
from the top floor of our old house,

glass buildings winking on
their peninsula beyond the water's thumb—

we passed the unexpected holiday
bringing each other cups of tea,

swapping perfumed latherings
with the new Christmas soap, and reading

recipes and poems alternately
aloud from our new Christmas books.

All afternoon was brilliant, as light is
only when refracted off of snow.

Later, we donned skis and braved
the cold, wanting to watch the sun

go down beyond the woods.
                    To the east, the city's panes flamed

                                against the sky, and on our hill
                    white turned *rose*—a stand of birches

burned around us, and our life
                    together seemed a single flux

                                quickening below the bark,
                    a slim trunk radiant

                                against a field of snow.

The Keeper

When the keeper dies, you have
to tell the bees or they leave
their hive and hang, a ball of
hot thorns in a high tree,
and you can't get them down
with smoke or sugar. Mum said
give the ponies a flake of hay,
see if the hens have laid,
then take the eggs to the barn.
She wants me out of the house.
I bring our news to the hive, sorry
I'm late, we were busy and I
am busy. She wants me out
when they bring him down.
He's fat, the stairs turn twice
and the door is so skinny
our tree has to come through the window
at Christmas. She called
his name three times, I stood
outside the sound, and then
I didn't have to go to school.
Now they're bringing him
down on a board, she wanted me
out, they'll turn him sideways
to fit, I know. She said
give the roosters a pan of corn.
Meat roosters, so dumb
they peck their own cuts

for blood. Two are fighting, two
always fight, but King Max doesn't.
Tail full of green, he eats
seed from my hand. We'll
keep him sweet, Dad promised.

Tahoe City Hello Girls

for Eunice Henrikson, Myrt Carnell, Skippie Nilson,
and Mildred Ross, telephone operators in a Lake Tahoe
Tattler *newspaper photograph, 1943*

Girls, you are my mother's age.
I'm glad you spent the war back home,
nursing Tahoe's telephones.
That hat, Eunice (really more

a sort of turban than a hat)
sets you apart as slightly older than
your chums. You have those pregnant-looking
matron's hands, plump and swollen

slightly at the joints. Today
we'd recommend light exercise
and warn you off of salted nuts
and gin. Maybe Myrt (I wondered why

she holds her *Stage and Screen* an arm's-
length from her face) is fanning you?
That makes sense. You must have gotten
close in summer, when *The Tattler* tells

your switchboards winked nonstop with calls
for tourists coming in. Now,
speaking of closeness, Skippie, what is it
you're hiding behind that boyish name?

You look as un-butch as your pals . . .
perhaps just a touch of extra
padding in the shoulders of
your suit? Your nickname makes me think

you sauntered in ten minutes late
for every shift, singing *Hello
Girls! Hello Girls!* . . . Mildred,
with your Rita-Hayworth-ruby smile,

if you lost someone over there
I hope you keep his letters safe
where, in her day, your girl will find them,
awed you've secreted another life.

Grown

I didn't want to grow and have the work she had.
I was old enough to set the table: a glass of wine
marking her place, my own mug of wine and water
to learn on, laying the small-tined fork by my plate.

But she had to shift the clattering pots
crowding the stovetop, and stir the measured cornmeal
careful not to shush the water's rolling boil.
Without scalding her wrists, she soaked the fatty beads

off the broth by dabbing breadcrusts on its skin.
The cheese fell to her hand's stronger circles
against the grater's graveled side. When you are grown
you buy the salt, the oil, the wine. When you

are grown you type letters in an office to buy
whatever you can't raise. Come home from work,
you take off your uncomfortable shoes. Some nights
you hold a sobbing child and sing *Papa's*

Gone a' Hunting, rocking in the wicker chair.
Or tie a stiffened apron over your oldest clothes.
I did not want that work. Grown meant alone.
The father wasn't coming back, and you were left

the hunter of rabbits. Red flecking your cheeks,
you'd carry a covered basket from their hutch.
A blade along each throat would stop their cries,
your only help a girl, flinching, blood-shy.

The Alembic

Could you stop burning long enough
                    to observe these women
            widowed from desire,
        retired to twin solitudes
                        below a single roof,

you would learn the truth
                    embodied here:
            the end of happiness
        marks the beginning of peace.
                        Now they govern a sphere

subaqueous and crystalline. Minute
                    bubbles of air adhere
        along each surface. Rare
            visitors permitted to submerge
                        likewise have silver facets,

expire their own filigrees
                    of breath. Yet none acquired
        this mineral tranquillity
            coolly, though at last
                        they are pacifically composed.

They were refined in the alembic —
                    first ardor's heat:
        champagne drunk
                    from Mason jars, its prickling, gingered bite;
                a firefly

alight within the trumpet
                    of a lily; the Perseids
        lapping an August night.
                Then sorrow's distillate:
                            years of loneliness

which also burned,
                    until it chilled
        and in them turned
                to that keen tincture
                        where peace begins.

"Hunter's Moon,"

                my mother calls the golden fist
clenched above the rye stubs, half-gloved in smoke haze
over our burning fields.

Mine remains the smaller hand. No blood yet,
my bones not begun reaching for a woman's height
while her body, digging

late onions from the frost-line at the garden's
ashen foot, seems strong as if my birth
had never broken her.

Three rabbits, bold after a summer of plenty,
don't hesitate as we unearth the row. Sleek, they take
all hunger makes its own.

II

A Portrait

In memory of Alba Lavezzo Flanagan

In summer, her supper was dependable:
cottage cheese and canned pears
I had a standing invitation to share
when tripe or other inedibles
appeared on the family table.

Should I look sallow, she cried
Milk of Magnesia the remedy,
chalky teaspoons I balked at, bribed
by the rustling of *After Eight Mints*.
The knob of her radio fixed with a band-aid

permanently to "her station,"
we'd work through a box of chocolates,
watching moths collect on the door
as if they, too, were listening for
the thrilling, hollow racket of strikes

bowled on *Candlepins for Cash*.
Before bed she wrapped her hair in a net,
then moved her pillow to the mattress's foot
so that waking each morning her eyes first glimpsed
a wedding portrait of the Kennedys

cut from the Sunday paper and framed.
Declaring herself a "lapsed Catholic"
she one day wrapped her rosary beads

away in an empty tin, and never again
brought them out. The sash of her purple robe

bore singes along one angled tip:
more than once I saw her use it
as a brand to light her stove.
For a while, we wrote each other letters—
my stories from college, her magazine clips,

commentary crammed along the margins
in her prickly, canted hand.
Blind her last six months, she died
"of boredom" at one hundred and one.
It was August, and took two weeks

before the message reached me
across country. *The Boston Globe,*
news that could no longer spark
her views, arrived until the year's end
each morning on her stoop.

The Sisters

i. Earliest Church

North End, Boston 1910

Before I was old enough to work beside my parents
in their store, the staved oak barrels they bought
cheaply from the dustman, who had swapped them
with the brewer's boy, who had stolen them off the hops-
cellar steps on Charter Street, were my earliest church.

Never mind Pick Alley's famed coal chutes, yawning for eggs.
You could keep the wharf rat—big as a terrier—
caught on North Pier, while the first knuckle of Ita Galassi's
twisted left hand, measuring caraway seed like shavings
of gold into her sausage, meant nothing to me.

Even my beautiful sister, returning from summer spent
among wealthy girls at the shore, prodigal with her trunk
full of shells and marlin-twine and shards of glass
from shattered Wingershiek light, and her souvenir
Guide to Racing Semaphore (with color plates), could wait.

Over our shop, the sign should've read *Lavezzo's*
Epiphany Peaches and Christmas Rose Grapes. Or
B. Lavezzo, Kentucky Wonder Melons & Plushpelt Pears.
For such names people would brave August heat on Prince
                                                    Street,
their business feathering our ledger's wings, and Papa

every morning would clip on his watch-chain and walk me
the long way down Hanover to school, nodding at everyone
raising their hats. Unitarian ladies from Back Bay
and Cambridge and even Beacon Hill would crook their
                                                    ankles
in a pollen-dusted foxtrot down the aisles

amid our coopered domes of gilded rind, mink smell
drowned in orchard perfume, murmuring *Seedless Flame
. . . Sultan's Turban . . . Bountiful Queen . . .* When winter
shoved in off the Atlantic and shod the city in slush,
Mayor Honey Fitz, the Saturday before his re-election,

would climb atop a polling booth at Fanueil Hall.
Top button of his collar undone, he'd sweep
his detractors and swoon pearl-throated
ladies to their knees by crooning "Sweet Adeline"
in open homage to my father's *Elephant Heart Plum.*

ii. Charity

The Saturday Evening Girl's Club, Beacon Hill, 1913

Tea with cream is sweet after a supper of sausage at home.
Below the parlor's electric light, each girl's scrubbed fingers
barely press the edge of her eggshell-thin bone china cup
against her lips. Fine ladies never gulp, they learn, never
                                                        reach
across with their spoons. Wearing a ring starred with
                                        marcasite,
the hostess pours each girl a second cup while her maid
offers them gingerbread the cook has baked to look
like happy men. The youngest girl would like one, yes.
She lays aside her scissors and thread, curling her hands
to hide their scabs. Violet-scented by the washroom's
perfumed soap, her sister's hands seem white as a lady's
beside her. Spines tensed to rods, the girls sew:
eight needles stabbing twenty stitches to an inch
in the yards of bleached cotton patterned into gowns
for colored mothers' laying-in. The stitching makes her
                                                    dreamy.
Now and then a suck of breath when someone pricks a
                                            finger.
Cloth sags loosely to the carpet like the pear's skin
her father unwound in gold hoops with a knife. Soft fruit
won't sell, they eat it themselves or give it to the Seamen's
                                                    Home.
Down the salted cobblestones of Beacon Hill,
across the Common's silence from the warm house
where she sews, there waits a box of spotty apples
on the juice-stained counter of their shop. Her father

crushes newspaper, making pockets of air. With him,
she'll wrap every apple. The blind man at the Home
won't see the crate her father brings, but he'll bend to
a crouch and breathe from the seams, bow to the voice
and say *We Thank You, Sir.*

iii. The Spinster and the Wife

Bay Road, 1923

Money came to our tenement monthly
tucked in envelopes of laid
sent by rich ladies whose houses sat back
off the street. All saying
An ailing girl gains strength
from a month of breakfasts
eaten on a sanded porch
the same good women one summer took
my beautiful sister with them to Wingershiek
wearing a new blouse piped like a sailor's.

There she learned to steer a skiff
full of Cape Cod girls, her braid
blown out behind them, black enough
to brighten the pinnacled clouds.
She found her beauty.
Below her shoes, the bay's tongue lapped salt
stung with lobster floats,
and at night she learned nothing
escapes the water's wink and spit,
tossing the lighthouse back its sparks.
She dreamt:

> *In bleached sheets before sleep I row*
> *the ocean's each pocket, at last*
> *slick with periwinks aslip in my gaze as,*
> *become the deep water,*
> *marlin tars me*

smoke to the beam. Become the gull's
bladed beak through picked gills, then I'm
the herring's gill itself, packed and torn,
blood into blossom, waking first
plumed in the house of dreaming girls.

She grew too fine. At summer's end
she came back to the city, but so beautiful
she never truly came back, and I
in her stead am the sister who married.
Private, she tends our father's dwindled house.

Wait—let me keep one summer of whiteness!
Chaperoned beneath a parasol, I still
burned brown! Two freckles
mark a place the milk-boy wants to kiss
but never will.

Letter to a Best Friend

My Dear G. —
        what a shame there's no place
in our "grown-up" lives for those guests
           we once loved to have visit, where conversation
interrupted years ago might revive, sugared by
        a sweet nostalgia for that past (spiked
with gratitude things didn't actually last
           any longer than they did!) Don't you wonder, now,
what became of the man you almost married
           that summer I bought my red dress and caused
minor havoc of my own? Remember his basket
        full of no-longer-ornamental bittersweet
you refused to throw out, strewing little cupped petals
        glumly across our table for weeks?
I'd hang my bathing suit over the branches to dry.
           Didn't you say he wrote you a confessional
letter after his last honeymoon, from France? Well,
        smart you broke the engagement then.
Though he was a charmer at parties — the one man
           who could dance . . . I recall a number of his
                      stories, too
(he always seemed in racy trouble, somehow)
           and must've thought he'd better entertain his gal's
best friend, on the off-chance you'd get cold feet
           and need my feminine push. And that weekend
rained under in Maine, when he taught us both to read
        the i-ching! It is a good thing you didn't marry him,
        but still, imagine sitting down and hearing

his version of the tale—not just your evaporated
nuptials and what, or if, he thinks now of that summer—
            but everything that's happened since.
                                    It's odd,
      I really don't think I considered him a separate
            person then at all: he was merely your lovely
bauble, another cultured pearl added to
            our glowing, opera-length necklace of pals.
      Yet I can picture him now distinctly, talking
            on that telephone we kept in the hall.
My own amours in those days surely called
            their families as well, but they're complex in
my memory, and refuse to pose for easy scenes . . .
            I wonder if he'd remember an old fiancé's
closest friend, several weddings, several lifetimes'
            dramas back? Could we chat simply as people
      enjoying catching up, who'd barely touched
            each other long ago, except in that once-
removed intimacy adoring *you* loaned to *us*, that part
      we shared gladly, where we knelt to bestow
      our differently voiced devotions at your heart?

Magician's Anniversary

Sixty years ago
he first kissed her,
turning her lips to goldfish
with ragged lace fins,

and tonight he reaches across
the board where he shaves the cheese,
slips his finger
slender as a lamb's tongue
in her ear, and pulls out

a nuthatch, which flies to the window
above the wooden table
where she slices a fat onion
and weeps.

Old Story with a Flowered Hat

From the docks a day below Chiavari the woman walks
past coils of pitch-soaked rope already sweating smoky resin,
past spitting, broken-fingered men gliding their knives
along the bellyseams of ripe sardines. Through new-paved
                                                    streets
she walks, streets new and new piazzas, the Corso
Garibaldi, past empty niches she remembers
holding saints.
                And out of the city, hotter as noon's haze
swallows the sea that hangs behind, she leads the girl
lagging and damp through her traveling dress's layered skirts.
They are slowly passing fields where years ago
the woman spent her afternoons in harvest time, goats
driven by a boy who whistles so as not to stare
passing with grass-stained bells and blinkless brassy eyes.

By dusk they have reached the stream's musical boundary
outside the mountain farm. At the gate, whose loosened nails
grant the horizontal rails a weathered slant,
the woman stops, and pausing
                            takes off her flowered hat
because age has made her mother blind and her father
will not recognize an American twenty years after
she sailed to Boston, a passage bride
wearing a stranger's name and a braid down her back.

At last, when she is older even
than the speechless silver man who knelt
bringing his daughter's creased palms to his cheek,

my grandmother passes me
the hat's starched roses crushed in her mother's hand

long after that hand, the weeping man, the girl who climbed
all day have passed us and gone
back to the start.

How to Get to Sleep

Go along the stone porch, up the two
　　　　　narrow steps to her hall. Into half-darkness.
　　She was old already when you were small.
　　　　　　　Walk on newspaper away from the back
　　　　　　　　　　　room's

stacked linoleum and the wooden
　　　　　unmeshed frames of screens.
　　Paint in lidless cans grown a skin
　　　　　of rubber. Past bridles looped on hooks,

their rust-flecked bits, to her kitchen.
　　　　　She lived until you left here.
　　Look for the towel she hung
　　　　　over the green-pocked glass

of her window. Look for the west's
　　　　　red cut through the pines.
　　The lamp is amber and the thin
　　　　　cracked glaze of every plate

wiped clean. Her fan's magnetic
　　　　　drone lulls the house. On boards
　　your feet are silent, bare. You pass
　　　　　between rooms, walls, in shadow,

unseen. In summer she slept downstairs,
              a sheet cooling the wool of her couch.
       This is how to get to sleep. New leaves
                     stirring beyond the screen door

and the shutters propped open for air.
              This is how you get to sleep.
       No dust shrouds the mirror. No light
                     but the moon's daguerreotype there.

They Lived Here

In a backwards accident,
men cutting the old furnace
out to make room for oil
find the wedding band
that slipped, in February
nineteen twenty-four,
down the heat vent and melted
to a coal. It was the coldest
month of the year my mother
was born, and the Captain
sat quiet while his wife,
her hands dressed in pie-flour
and girlish without
the gold reminder, cried.
No one who was there
the night my grandmother
lost the ring her husband
brought her on *The Daisy*
from Brazil is still alive.
Not Fernstrom, the giant
neighbor whose crowbar pried up
the iron grill, nor his wild sons
Mack and Theo, carrying
an orchard ladder crusted with ice
into the parlor and fighting
over who would climb
down the galvanized duct.
Not Duchess, the terrier

of wiry hair and almost
human reason who patrolled
the hole's edge, and then,
barking, led the men to the cellar
where they swear she scratched
at the belly of the coal box
as if she could smell gold.
The Captain, singed by the lamp's
hot kerosene as he hammered
to loosen the fuel bin's floor,
is dead. Even my grandmother,
walking without coat or shawl
on the dark porch, her hand's
misshapen fingers pressing
a snowball to her eyes,
is gone. She told stories
like this one. Mostly
I believe they were true,
although she lied once
to my mother. She said
the Captain went singing,
quick to heaven. My mother
was small, there was a stroke.
She didn't know her father
wandered out to Prince's
stall and took the broken
harness down, making Prince
mouth the rusted bit, then
gave him sugar for working
hard all day at the plough.
Her father used a pick
to clean each hoof, pulling

loose the horseshoes over
hooves he dug raw.
A girl that age would hardly
remember a father at all,
so her mother lied:
he went quick to heaven,
singing. But one thing
my mother saw was the barn step
as she fell, and a man
who ran with her to the house.
Her eyes, she was cut, he was
blurred red but she saw blue
eyes and the sleeve of his coat
a black, rough blue. She knew
she hurt because he cried,
running so fast she felt warm
in her blood. That must have been
her father. He held her
open head against the wool.

III

A Late Apostasy

for D.

Roaming the Via degli Alfani
late each night, I pass Saint Sebastian
swooning in arrow-stricken ecstasy
from his quattrocento niche. Christ's passion
sweetened the pricks so their piercings ached like lips
against his beating skin. My charismatic
apostle of more secular erotic trips,
you've grown apocryphal as this fantastic
martyr who wrecks me with his brimming eyes.
Half-jesting, I drew hearts transfixed by arrows
across my first envelopes to you. Jokes die
like saints, we found: they leave hard-to-swallow
legends, illuminating our naive
supplication to a god we once believed.

Nostalgie de la Boue

He told me the first time they made love
he undressed her completely
                              except for a scarf
she'd wrapped twice round her waist as a belt,
rind-yellow linen, and later when she slept
he slid the tangle from her hips
and stretched it over her: a sail
to gather her smell.
                              He kept it
all the years they lived
together in the foreign city, kept it still
when she came home to marry
someone else. She has a second child,
he's heard through friends. The city
they found themselves exotic in
is spoiled for him by loud Americans,
and the scarf bears new seams each time
he rends it—then weakening, stitches the tear.

To a Paleolithic Boy in His Grave

The small mouth of a hole curls around you:
you are its bent tongue refusing to speak.
Small Mouth, someone bundled you in grasses,
nesting your sides in a cradle of buds
I imagine were picked for their promise,
removing them from promise.
Perhaps your mother lay you here
after winding the beaded hide you wear
about your hips. But why did she wrap you?
Was it warmth for the winter you'd sleep among seeds
before rising in spring as a man? Or raiment
so you needn't stand poorly at the altar
but come shawled for your goddess-bride
expectant in the halls of earth? Because,
Small Mouth, I cannot bear the thought
your mother tried to wake you among blossoms
but could not. Killed a fawn in your place
and shaped its skin around you, saying
Now he will walk to me on the legs of a deer.
You did not walk. You lay changed as your mother
sat, shocked, alongside you. As any mother
by her child's strange body must wait. No grief
swallows her yet at your silence. No belief
a small mouth in the earth could unname you.

Punte Sotillo, 1942

From a photograph

The soldier facing left and wearing a peaked hat
is my father. His right hand holds an orange
he's peeled and begun to eat. His vanished life
still shows, if you know to look
for the stain of the paint's blue grease below his nails,
the hair singed off his fingers by the kiln.
He skipped an adze down the bone steps
of his knuckles once, carving boxes as a boy.

Though darkened in the photograph,
the olive skin of the south
can't hide how the war has marked him:
his thumb, an artist's thumb,
bruised now by the gun's recoil.

The Body of Speech and Silence

i.

The Egyptians believed the intelligence
lived alongside the soul in the heart.

Least-valued of organs, the brain
was withdrawn after death by small hooks

thrust into the skull through each nostril,
extracting soft tissues while leaving the profile

intact. Once the stomach, intestines,
and lungs, all needed in the afterlife,

were lifted through the clean abdominal slit
and dressed in gum-soaked linen

studded with amulets, they were packed
with natron in the waiting canopic jars

bearing the heads of the sons of Horus.
Inside the sarcophagus of faience

over gilded wood, the desiccated heart
lay stitched within the body's cavity,

from which the gods' tribunal
would pluck it to measure its worth.

ii.

There is an epilepsy so severe
        the afflicted never live an hour
                free of seizure. Against sublimity—
        that blazing world outside our bodies
our bodies mediate—stand only
        the brain's synapses, dimming
                sensation to bearable flares. And when
        these microscopic shades are singed?
Surgeons open the skull with a saw.
        Cradled within the porous bone, the brain pulses
                homely gray. Deep below the cerebral
        cortex, damaged nerves spark
incendiary storms. When the corpus callosum
        linking the globed hemispheres
                is deftly cut, the child
        electrocuted by her own senses
lives cooled, no longer the struck
        body of too many voices
                burning to speak through one mouth.

iii.

In the story of his death, Shelley's body,
washed to the beach with Keats's poems
folded still in his left breast pocket, is given to flames on the
                                                                sand.
Friends watch his bones through the blaze and see them
char to the friable white of ash. And then one mourner cries
Look there! Look!
                    Where was Mary Shelley's mind
before that shout and the man plunging his gloved hand
through the husk of her husband's ribs?
Walking the iron plain of an arctic sea.
How is it these silent parts make up a man?
she asks when they hand her the handkerchief
wrapping his heart, which refused to burn.

iv.

Shall I tell you the saddest of myths?
　　　　　On the third day the women went
　　　weeping to the tomb and saw
　　　　　　the rock had been moved aside.

Upon entering, they found the body of the Lord
　　　　　was missing and, fearing thieves,
　　　sent up a cry. And the Lord,
　　　　　　building hell's bridges of bone,

could hear them.
　　　　　But had no tongue.

v.

In the underworld
it will be Annubis, the jackal-headed god,
who asks for my heart. The points of his golden scale
prick the green sky, and I'll waver,
not given yet to either world
as he balances my life's unfinished gravity
against a feather.

The Better Half of Man

L'erbe "Voglia" non cresce mai nel giardino del Re

The flower called *I Want* blooms not
       within the gardens of Paradise,
nor do its roots number here

       among Purgatory's narrow beds
where the soul descended
       cleanses itself with soil and a rake.

To accompany his loneliness,
       one newcomer sings lullabies
until stilled by the lettuces'

       indifference to song.
The flower called I Want blooms not . . .
       These phrases of his mother

carried over the water
       wither, so he buries them
beside the onion. The onion,

       whose single word is a copper bolt
demanding tears. In this middle world,
       day is ever day without change,

night is ever night. What he feels
       lisping as time is his tongue
returning its verbs.

Across the mullioned greenhouse
walls, his image flashes
          and he perceives he's slow

becoming a creature
          half-man, half-wheelbarrow—
the better half of each.

          The better half of man
is silent, and the barrow
          bears his load. Without voice,

he grows a purer ear
          for the thorns' cry, *Hold me.*
Within, his last worldly

          solace of poise
is torn—*Human, weep*—
          by the onion's plangent command.

From a Table at the Forest's Edge

The flagstones were sunken in the grass and partially
grown over. They were glittering with dew
the sun hadn't yet lifted, so the center
of the meadow pronounced itself
articulate from the shadow
confusing the wood's edge. In that lit middle
my father stood beside a table
spread with flaxen cloth.
He was dead and offered me wolf apples
from an oak bowl. Our lexicon
formed itself of gazes and scent:
flecks of mica winking up from the stones,
a peppery cider spiked the air.
One apple bore a pair of waxy leaves
notched at the edges like delicate teeth,
and slender russet fibers veined the flesh
where my bite left its white mark.

Elegy for My Father

Maybe he sings in a heaven of consolations.
Still, I'd prefer him failing and lonely
and alive. Crossing the bridge in the Public Garden

each day he'd watch children, subdued
by parents or jostling in twos and threes,
packed on the Swan Boat's slatted benches.

A limber, sunburnt boatman would sit
between the swan's wings on a seat
cast from rough metal, and paddles

skirted below the syrup of brown water
would guide the swan in figure-eights
past two islands with their complaining

families of mallards and Canada geese.
In September, trees by the bridge begin dropping
coin-sized leaves on the water. The swans

glide through, skimming dark fans.
Before the weather turned
and the boatdock was housed away,

without a child to urge him, he'd pay
the keeper for a ticket and almost enjoy
the half-abandoned swan, a goose's arguments.

IV. Nostos

The city is built
To music, therefore never built at all,
And therefore built for ever . . .

Votive to the Genius of Place

Palazzo Ginori, Florence

Offering:

Allegro: meaning cheerful, merry, bright.
    As in music, often
the first movement played, to draw us forward
    in our seats. As in
the curtain across the way—blue, a genial ruffle
    bobbing on updrafts
from the piazza below. Behind it sleep
    a woman and a man, who
every afternoon, knowing they are nearly
    the highest window
above the square, make love leaving the blue
    half-drawn. Perhaps it's air
they want about them, perhaps it's light.
    When he wakes, the man
walks naked to their kitchen, pours water
    from a bottle, drinks part
walking back, then sets her half beside the bed.
    Or, a variation:
the hour belled in the campanile
    stirs her first and she
gets up. The one glass shared between them
    is the constant note.
Not far from here, a saint keeps watch over
    the crossroads. Once
I found him mournful, pegged high on the wall
    above a shelf littered
with offerings of failing petals and spilled wax,

cigarettes stamped to sponge
buds along the wood. His bound hands, his swoon,
    the arrows shot through
his crudely painted wounds all stabbed me
    with awkward empathy.
Yet I know Sebastian burned for death.
    He defied an emperor
and fell, ecstatic, crying his passion to
    the sky above the ditch.
We're meant to read the chipping plaster
    tears as tears of joy.
Outside the lovers' window, a cat stretches
    belly-up along
two terracotta tiles jutting over
    forty feet of pigeon-
scented air, her eye-seams tight shut against the sun,
    basking while her keepers fuck.

Genii:

And what will you make of these Visions, o Human
We Guardians have chosen as Witness to our Bliss?

To Vertumnus

He's no world traveler, roaming here or there,
But knows the neighboring hills like his right hand.
                              —Ovid, Metamorphoses

i.

October sun answers the visitor's query,
lightly resolving why all the city's walls
are painted shades of yellow: by contrast
they heighten heaven, as gold tracing the pleats
lends a painted virgin's robe its depth.
Into that blue climbs the market's copper roof.
An artist studying the feral cats that flourish
atop the houses could scale its slope to watch.
Even from my lower perch, I spy one of the tribe
on her afternoon hunt. At a rainpipe's dislocated joint
she sniffs, then lowers gingerly into pose. When I cluck
across the piazza, she doesn't break her crouch to look,
but flicks me the flattened inside of her nearest ear.
It translates clearly as a human finger to the lips.

ii.

As the sun sets in November, it's easy to see
why there are so many yellow buildings here.
Licked by cirrus flames, the smelter's cauldron sky
casts the walls in gold with its furnace light.
That line of clerestory windows, burnished
just below the market's copper roof, must show
the evening star a rose-lensed kaleidoscope
of fruitstands and slowly milling heads below its slope.

Now on the roof next door, Signora Qualcuno
tucks in her tiny garden for the night.
She thins the rows of lettuce growing under frames
and diapers a dwarf Something-tree's roots
in plastic wrap—it's too dark to see its leaves or fruit.
The bulb above her sputters giddily with gnats.

iii.

December, when the fog burns off, I remember why
so many buildings are painted yellow here. Outside,
behind the rooves, the clouds resemble hammered tin.
Gilt-foil walls, a balcony's wrought-iron rail.
The old sacristy dome of San Lorenzo flashes
tiles lapped like fishscales, neat enough to number
had I time to count the details of the view.
                                        Noon.
A quiet that, in retrospect, seems presciently still
breaks like water's face at the first rock of church bells—
San Lorenzo, San Gaetano, Santa Maria del Fiore,
the other two Saint Marys (Novella and Maggiore)
—all set by different watches. For ten minutes, the hour
ripples across town. Time slows down. Or
picks up, *is picked up*, multiplied by the lead tongues.

iv.

In January, while the gutters rush with water, I try
recalling the houses' sunlit yellow walls. Against my window
rain rain go away blurs the oily glass.
One smear of light floats where the covered market
vanished into fog. A train passing Campo Marte
tosses off its virile hoot, but only the frailest wheezing
travels through the wet. Even the hawker's barrows
trundled from the piazza splash, as if the swollen river
has cobbled the alley with fish. Overhead, busy
scratching in between the rooftiles and the ceiling
sifts a mist of plaster faintly down around my chair.
They say rats abandon doomed ships before they sink.
Damp as it is, then, at least this ark is watertight . . .
or so my upstairs neighbors seem to think.

v.

No fallen February snow to cast weak light
back at the walls' yellow, for days no sun
lifts their tinges above jaundice and tallow.
The green market-roof looks patina'd with mildew.
Carneval came and went. Now Lent hangs
its penitential shroud over the darkened streets.
Yet one law, older than punishment, commands:
these dawns, I've woken to a pair of swallows
whistling as they nest above my window ledge.
And today, discarded on the sill, I found
a shell mosaic, tesserae of the precise design
life itself broke through. I heard the vital,
piping brood and understood why the first Christians
fledged their Paraclete in the body of a bird.

vi.

Feste delle Donne

A change, a change altogether in March. High wind
wheels through the city, beating against the yellow walls,
shuddering windows in their frames so the market
itself, through the violently shaken glass, seems to tremble.
Not a cloud softens the sky or shadows the piazza
where broken stems of mimosa lie, blown from the golden
sprays
hung on every shop-door in honor of the feast.

Birds screel above, whipped by the unseen element.

Across the street, the invalid who thought she'd never greet
another spring sits at her windowsill. A gust
eddies her remaining hair. From here I watch her effort,
her shoulders heft and lowered with each breath. Yet
she smokes a cigarette, whose ash and plume the invisible
wind scatters, matter returning through fire to air.

A Sight

The sun's return confounds the wet, which last night
        blew through winter's teeth
across the piazzetta and the bending elms glistening
        blue in ambulance light.

Medics crouched along the swimming cobblestones
        as I crossed the road
on my midnight walk. When I returned, the rain had slowed.
        Ambulances gone,

the elms reclaimed obscurity above the park.
        Two policemen smoked
below a portico and there, where it was struck,
        lay a body sheeted white

except the nearest hand. It was too dark to tell
        details of age or sex
or if it wore a wedding ring. It feels obscene
        that I, with no idea

whose hand it was, should see its owner dead
        (and all night dream
our palms are drowned cups emptying)
        while now, in streaming sun,

someone who knew the hand might still prepare
        her morning coffee, woken
early by the vernal light and unaware
        anything's changed but the weather.

Epiphany

On the sixth of January, sun and birdsong wake me.
Befana, the hunchbacked crone of Epiphany
who leaves presents tucked in children's shoes
and, in exchange, carries the holidays off in her sack,
has kindly taken the winter storm, too.
As I lie on my belly planning the day's attack
I notice my shoulder's loosened skin sinking,
thin and wrinkled, into a muscled hollow.
When I pull with my finger gently along the bone,
more skin slackens into the shallow.
The lines on it are rayed, fine as snowflakes,
exquisite—then I realize the skin's *my own*.
Struck, I straighten the arm, and the sunken flesh
agrees for the time to resume its customary pose.

The Feast of San Silvestro

All week, the explosions have increased.
On Monday, three or four
startled the afternoon,

sending up a piazza-
ful of pigeons, their wings
clattering like water on stone.

Every car alarm
within fifty yards went off.
Tuesday, they gathered steam.

Rapid clusters seemed
normal by Wednesday,
and though lunchtime was sunny

we kept the windows shut,
afraid an ascending rocket would
set the curtains aflame.

After three, just when
a siesta beckoned to
freshen us for the feast,

some back-alley wits
blew up the metal
trashcans outside our

bedroom wall. God
        bless mankind! Whose
                youthful spirit, head

bowed in the temple of
        the festive muse, hath found
                toy elements—

thunder in a paper cup,
        gunpowder perihelions
                eclipsing with a

shriek. Listen, sweet,
        early tomorrow, while the
                infant deities

still sleep, we'll walk
        the river's edge to greet
                the year's first, foggy light

come stumbling over
        the celestial
                shards sodden in the street.

La Colpa

The man is quarreling with someone. He sits
       on the roof outside his blue-curtained window,

shouting into a cellular telephone
       so that across the piazza I hear him insist

E la tua colpa! La tua! to whomever
       holds the other end. I've never seen him

clothed before. Oddly, it makes him seem
       stranger than glimpsing him carelessly naked

through his open windows ever has.
       Who's responsible? What have they done

to transform him from the attentive god
       cradling his lover's legs atop the pillows

into this man, phone pinched
       between shoulder and ear, twisting his watchband

until the face catches sunlight and flashes
       silver against his wrist like a little blade?

And why do his words, spat from a rooftop
       in this foreign drama, cut? They're familiar enough

though we aim the blow in other terms—
       Your fault, it's your fault, it's yours.

Zephyrus

If winter comes, can spring be far behind?
           —Shelley, "Ode to the West Wind"

Gray, swaying, and slender, their bare
parasol-ribs laced high overhead,
the poplars along the river don't offer
much shelter. But the wind
no longer smells quite like winter wind.
Through the Cascine where we walk
it carries draughts of mud and,
I'm certain, cows—beyond the city,
sheltered beneath cedars on the lee-
side of some Tuscan hill, or maybe it's
the dung of seventeenth-century cows
risen through the thawing earth
as ghostly perfume from earlier days
when the park was a Medici dairy.
(It's my imagination, you insist,
or an especially verdant rats' nest
littered in the sedge along the bank.)

One rat startles us,
shooting sleekly from a burrow
nearly under our feet. It scoots
to the water's edge and back,
wearing the same oiled-looking pelt
as its history-book relatives,
probably home to the same type of flea
the plague bacteria liked as their host.
During the summer of 1348,

every third person
living in the city died.
Corpses washed up on the bank where we stand.
Now from folding chairs
lined along the gravel, old men fishing
nod to us as we pass.

Back on the pavement, bicycles zip.
One father and son are riding tandem.
The grown-up son wears thick glasses
and a helmet stenciled with butterflies.
He pedals fast and loudly sings,
leaving vowels like bubbles thinned
and fading in the air, and I
feel hollowed by his babbled song
which sounds eternal, the wordless
under-voice of the world's verses,
murmured . . .
                    This Romantic meditation's
drummed asunder by a maelstrom's
thunderous wave: a tide of roller-skaters
approaches—overtakes—
engulfs us with a shuddering surge,
then we are left awash
among the stragglers reeling in its wake.
At the walkway's border
out of all this hectic traffic's path,
grandparents push babies so swaddled
only their squeezed, hot-looking
faces show. The babies seem
older than we do, made of an ageless,
regenerate wax. Any afternoon
here throughout the last millennia

the same fathomless eyes
would have held our gaze, or blinked away.

They seem much older than
the modern hippodrome, whose amplified
bawl from the park's tip reverberates.
Even before we reach the grandstand's
scrubby rise and squint across
the hedge to catch the race, we hear
a crackling static exclamation as
Numero Seidieci takes the lead.
Each surrey floats low
behind its trotting horse, whose breath,
strained by the fourth lap, purrs
damply in its nose. You think
the surreys look like roman chariots.
I say they're flimsier than that—
if they resemble anything
from this city's past, it's those
inventions Leonardo sketched,
wings of canvas and rabbitskin
stretched over flexible rods.
                              (Were those wings
"flimsier" than a chariot? you ask—
The marble Empire's fallen, but now we fly!)

Most of the horses are clipped
for racing, coats trimmed close
along the body where they sweat,
their legs left feathered
in reddish winter down.
Soon they'll all begin to shed.
Toothmarked mats of hair, golden

chestnut and coppery bay, knocked
by the grooms from packed currycombs,
will blow across the trailer yard
to tangle in fences and weeds.
Birds, returning, will line their nests
with hair against the spring nights' chill.

Cold from standing still, we walk
back along a different path
threading a boggy soccer field.
You ask if crocus grows here,
and just as I'm about to answer
No, we spot one blooming at your feet.
Palest violet-white, its petals
are translucent, though when we crouch
and you tilt its cup toward us
we see the yellow center, vital
as a yolk. Others press
up through the bleached grass.
Stirred by the first warmth, these
are the youngest things in the park.
From what ancient papery bulbs
have they sprung?
                    I won't tell you
what goes through me at their sight;
not ready, quite, for your witty reply,
I don't, out loud, invoke

> *Long after our love and arguments are gone,*
> *May these rooted knobs still multiply*
> *Here where we stood, their petals scintillate*
> *In the changed wind's perennial eye.*

Adagio Ma Non Troppo

Golden-throated birds, their ripe warbling
        fluid as the new oil pressed from the olives,
        welcome dawn to my neighbors' courtyard
by scrabbling through a plastic sack of trash.

        Giving the junk a picking-over, they uncover
evidence of that eternal act once
celebrated by Etruscan lovers here:
        three condoms—all one night's work? I wince

as a starling stabs his horned claw through,
        gets caught, then pecks frantically to untie
        his ridiculous, monumental shoe.
What a parody of how desire dies!

        But the wife downstairs, to whom the trash belongs,
        warbles nightly, proving me wrong.

Notes

"Clever and Poor" is for Ruth Pelizzon.

The lines "the end of happiness / marks the beginning of peace" in "The Alembic" are adapted from a passage in Shaw's *Heartbreak House*.

"Letter to a Best Friend" is for Gaiana Germani.

L'erbe Voglia non cresce mai nel giardino del Re, a remark made to quiet a grumbling child, means "The flower called *I Want* doesn't even grow in the King's garden."

"The city is built to music . . ." is from Tennyson's *Idylls of the King*.

"To Vertumnus": Vertumnus is the Roman god of the changing seasons. The epigraph is from Horace Gregory's translation.

Zephyrus is the west wind. Shelley's "Ode to the West Wind" was composed in part on the poet's walks through the Cascine in Florence.

The "Nostos" poems are for Tony Deaton.